Illustrated History of
MARTIAL ARTS

JUDO

by Kevin K. Casey

illustrated by Jean Dixon

THE ROURKE CORPORATION, INC.
VERO BEACH, FL 32964

ACKNOWLEDGMENTS

I am grateful to Jean Dixon for her art and for her research in order to produce the painting of Jigoro Kano. I also thank Sensei Ray Meier and the Bushido-Kan Martial Arts Academy.

PHOTO CREDITS

All photos © Kevin K. Casey

Library of Congress Cataloging-in-Publication Data

Casey, Kevin, 1967-
    Judo / by Kevin Casey.
       p.   cm. — (Illustrated history of martial arts)
      Includes index.
      ISBN 0-86593-369-3
      1. Judo—Juvenile literature. [1. Judo.] I. Title. II. Series.
GV1114.C37   1994
796.8'152—dc20
                                      94-4090
                                        CIP

PRINTED IN THE USA
                                        AC

1

ORIGINS OF

J U D O

Judo is a form of wrestling from Japan. The word "judo" means "gentle way." In the 20th century judo has been practiced as a sport, but it originated hundreds of years ago as a dangerous, even deadly, type of combat.

In addition to training with swords, Japanese samurai warriors also trained in unarmed combat skills. One of the skills they trained in was called *taijutsu*, or "body art." Taijutsu was a form of fighting in which body leverage and quick movements were used to throw an attacker off-balance. Taijutsu later evolved into *jujitsu*. Most of the techniques in judo originated in the arts of taijutsu and jujitsu.

There are two main theories about the origin and development of Japanese unarmed body arts. One theory states that a Japanese doctor named Akiyama noticed how pine and willow trees weathered winter storms. The pine trees remained rigid and the weight of the snow often broke them. Willow trees were more flexible, and when they bent, the snow fell off of them, leaving them unharmed. Akiyama applied this knowledge to fighting.

TOKYO

Judo, taijutsu and jujitsu were developed in Japan. Today, the world headquarters of judo is located in Tokyo, Japan.

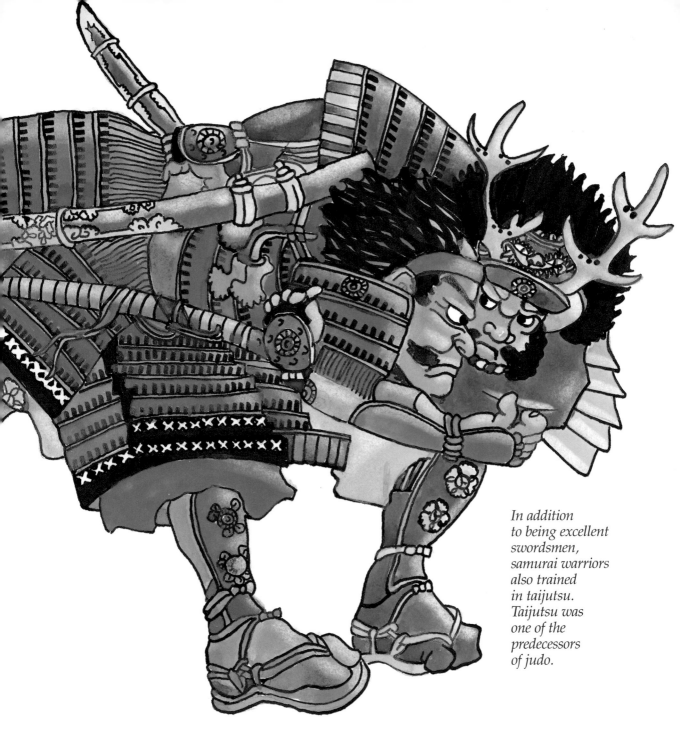

In addition to being excellent swordsmen, samurai warriors also trained in taijutsu. Taijutsu was one of the predecessors of judo.

The other theory states that Akiyama went to China to learn about medicine. While he was in China, he learned fighting skills from *kung fu* masters and brought the knowledge back to Japan.

Some historians reject both theories and say that taijutsu and jujitsu developed in Japan long before the life of Akiyama.

JUJITSU

The first known teacher of jujitsu was Hisamori Takenouchi. Takenouchi formed the first system of jujitsu in 1532. Like taijutsu and other earlier throwing arts, most of the techniques in jujitsu involved defeating opponents by forcing them to lose their balance. In many ways, jujitsu was a form of wrestling.

However, there was more to jujitsu than just wrestling. Jujitsu also included hand and arm strikes, joint locks, methods of strangulation, and kicking techniques. Early jujitsu was so dangerous that students had to be closely supervised because, unless they were careful, they might injure, or even kill, each other.

Some of the most effective – and dangerous – techniques in jujitsu are the joint-lock maneuvers. Early masters of jujitsu knew that the human body has many joints that can move only in certain ways. If pressure is applied so that the joints are forced in the wrong direction, the pain is so intense that a would-be attacker has to surrender, or receive more pain and maybe even serious injury.

Joint locks are an effective method of controlling a person. Police officers often use joint locks in order to subdue suspected criminals.

A person skilled in jujitsu can disable an opponent by throwing him off-balance. Some throws are so powerful that they can send an opponent flying through the air.

Other effective techniques in jujitsu are the nerve point strikes and the strangulation holds. Strikes to specific nerve points can temporarily paralyze an opponent's arms or legs. Strangulation holds cut off the air supply until the victim falls unconscious or dies.

3 JIGORO KANO

As a boy, Jigoro Kano was smaller than the rest of his classmates, and he was often sick. Almost every day, Jigoro Kano was bullied at school. He needed to learn a way to defend himself. When he was a teenager, Jigoro Kano began to study a type of jujitsu that concentrated on striking techniques. Later, Jigoro Kano changed schools and studied a type of jujitsu that emphasized throwing techniques.

Jigoro Kano continued to study jujitsu, and by 1883 he had learned enough that he began to teach others. Jigoro Kano called the style that he taught *kano-ryu*, or kano-style. Later the name was changed to *Kodokan* judo. The Kodokan was the first school of judo.

Jigoro Kano wanted to make judo a safe system so he eliminated all of the jujitsu techniques he thought were too dangerous. Other schools of jujitsu did not agree with the removal of dangerous jujitsu techniques, and to prove their point, they challenged members of the Kodokan to contests. The Kodokan members almost always won.

In 1886, a large tournament was sponsored by the Japanese police force. The Kodokan and all other major schools of jujitsu were invited. Jigoro Kano took his best students to the tournament, and they won 13 of their 15 matches. After the tournament, the Japanese government declared Kodokan judo an official martial art.

Jigoro Kano, the creator of judo, taught judo to many students in the late 1800s and early 1900s. His students won many contests.

THE FOUNDER OF JUDO

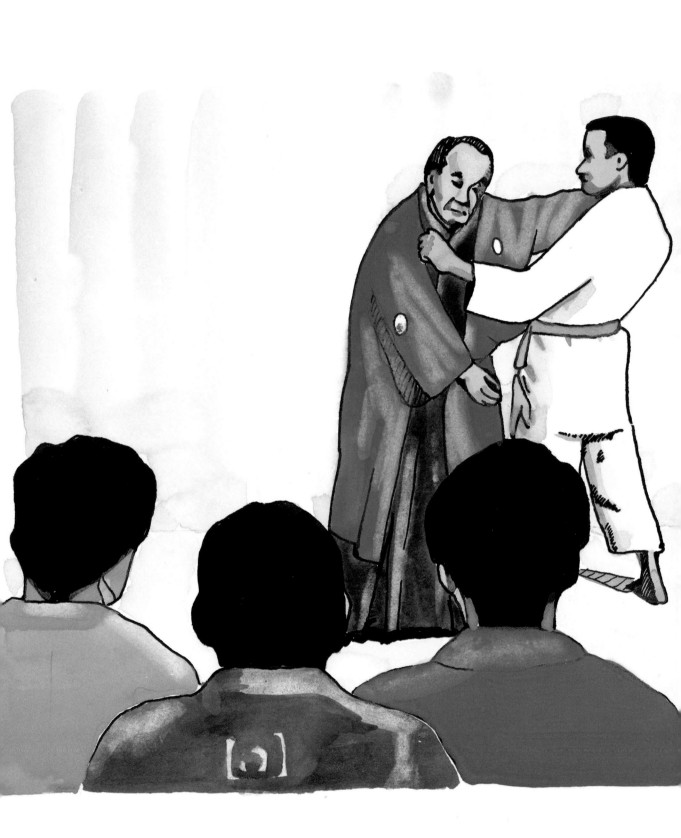

EARLY 20TH CENTURY

DEVELOPMENT

By the early 1900s, the Kodokan had become the most respected school of judo. There were still schools of jujitsu, but with the increase in popularity of Kodokan judo, the schools of jujitsu lost most of their influence.

In addition to being the founder of judo, Jigoro Kano was also a teacher. He believed that judo was an excellent form of physical education, and he persuaded many other teachers that it should be taught in public schools and colleges. The teaching of judo in the schools caused the popularity of judo to increase even more. Judo clubs gained more and more members.

In the first few years of the 20th century, judo was being taught to Japanese policemen. It was also taught to soldiers in the Imperial Japanese Army. Judo became an important part in every Japanese soldier's training.

Jigoro Kano continued to promote judo. In 1922, Jigoro Kano was given special recognition for his service to Japan. Jigoro Kano also helped to promote the Olympic Games. He died in 1938, while returning to Japan from Cairo, Egypt, where he had been meeting with the International Olympic Committee.

Jigoro Kano's former students continued to practice and teach Kodokan judo.

Early in the 20th century, judo was taught to Japanese college students, Japanese policemen, and soldiers in the Imperial Japanese Army.

OF JUDO

THE

S P R E A D

OF JUDO FROM JAPAN

Judo and jujitsu were the first Asian martial arts that became popular in the United States and Europe. In the early 1900s, there were many demonstrations of judo in Great Britain. Sometimes the Japanese judo experts would challenge British wrestlers. Often money was wagered, and the judo experts always won.

In other demonstrations, judo experts would let as many as seven men try to hold them down. It usually took only 20 seconds – or less – for the judo experts to escape. While demonstrations like these impressed the public, it took several more years for the British people to realize that judo was more than a series of gymnastic tricks. By 1911, judo was being taught to a few British army troops.

Judo was also becoming well-known in the United States. One reason for judo's increasing popularity was because of President Theodore Roosevelt. In 1902, Jigoro Kano sent a talented student from the Kodokan to be President Roosevelt's personal instructor. President Roosevelt had a room in the White House prepared for judo training, and he practiced regularly.

Police officers sometimes use this technique to remove unwilling suspects from automobiles.

7 THE DOJO

A school of judo is called a *dojo*. The judo teacher is called *sensei*. The student of judo is called a *judoka*.

Both teachers and students of judo wear a white uniform called a *gi*. A karate uniform is also called a gi. A judo gi looks like a karate gi but is much thicker and stronger. A judo gi must be strong because judo involves a lot of grappling and throwing. If the judo gi were not strong, it would tear.

Belts are used to designate rank. There are nine different colors of belts. The lower ranks, called *kyu*, are designated by white, yellow, orange, green, blue and brown belts. The upper ranks are called *dan*. The black belt is not the highest rank in judo. There are several higher grades, with two different belt colors. Those colors are red, and alternating blocks of white and red.

The floor of the dojo is covered with mats. The mats cushion the falls of students and help to prevent injury. Straw mats were used in traditional Japanese dojos but in modern dojos, as well as the Olympics, foam mats are used.

Here, a senior student throws a lower-ranking student. Modern dojos use foam mats to prevent injury and keep the practice of judo a safe and enjoyable sport.

Advanced students of judo are able to use powerful throws against opponents. In order to execute throws like this one safely, students of judo must practice often.

8

RANDORI AND KATA

Almost all judo training consists of *randori,* or free sparring. Free sparring permits two students to practice together. Each student is allowed to use any judo technique. Neither student knows which techniques the other will use. The object of free sparring is to throw one's opponent to the mat, just like in competition judo.

The practice of free sparring in judo training is the main reason that modern judo is more sport than martial art. In other martial arts, the various techniques are too dangerous to be used in free sparring, so all practice involving two students together is controlled, with both students performing rehearsed moves.

These two students are attempting to throw each other. This sort of training is especially useful in preparing for competition.

Most judo training is in the form of randori, or free sparring. Each student can use any legal technique in order to throw opponents to the mat.

There are milder versions of randori, in which both students know what technique will be used. The two students decide who will execute the technique. One student will then attempt to throw the other student. The student being thrown will cooperate so that the other can learn how to execute the throw. This type of randori is especially useful, because it permits two beginning students to help each other learn basic techniques.

Another form of judo training consists of *kata*, a series of rehearsed movements. Kata is useful in formal demonstrations of judo, as well as training in the dojo.

THE
B
R
E
A
K
F
A
L
L

The first thing that all students of judo must learn is how to fall without hurting themselves. In judo, the proper way to fall is called *ukemi*, or "breakfall." To understand the difference in a breakfall and an uncontrolled fall, think of the difference in a dropped egg and a dropped rubber ball. When an egg impacts with the ground, it breaks because it is rigid. When a rubber ball hits the ground, it bounces because it is flexible.

If a person's body is rigid, like an egg, the person may receive bruises, or even broken bones. If a person's body is flexible, like a rubber ball, it will not be hurt.

The student with the dark hair has just been thrown to the mat. Even though he has hit the mat with great force, he is not injured because he knows how to breakfall.

This student is practicing the backwards breakfall. Students of judo must learn this and other breakfalls before ever engaging an opponent.

One basic fall is the backwards breakfall. This breakfall begins in the standing position, with the student's arms outstretched, forward, at about face level. The head is tucked down, with the chin touching the upper chest. Then, the student drops, as if falling to a sitting position. Just before the buttocks impact with the mat, the student rolls backwards onto the back of the shoulders, while raising the legs. Immediately before the end of the roll, the student slaps the mat with both arms. This helps to further break the fall.

There are breakfalls that prepare a student for falling in any direction, whether it be forward, backward or sideways.

10

BALANCE AND SPEED

Maintaining balance is very important in judo. In competitive judo, the purpose of the various techniques is to throw the opponent off-balance and to the mat. This also applies to the self-defense aspects of judo. If opponents or attackers can be made to lose their balance, they no longer pose a threat.

Sometimes having the best balance is determined by something as simple as being closest to the ground. This is one of the reasons why almost any person, regardless of size or strength, can become skilled in judo. Other factors that determine balance are placement of the legs and feet, and control of the upper body. These are things that students of judo learn as they become more advanced.

Using balance and speed properly has allowed this student to throw a much larger opponent.

After forcing his opponent off-balance, this student easily throws his opponent to the mat.

Speed is another important factor in judo. The faster a technique can be executed, the more likely it will be successful. The longer it takes to execute a technique, the more time an opponent has to prepare and execute a counter move. This is why students of judo practice each technique over and over. The more the student practices, the faster the student can execute the technique.

11

LEVERAGE

One of the aspects of judo that sets it apart from other well-known martial arts is the throwing of opponents. Instead of punching or kicking an opponent or attacker, a person skilled in judo forces the opponent off-balance and then throws the opponent to the ground.

It is not uncommon for persons skilled in judo to be able to throw opponents much larger than themselves. In order to understand how this is done, it may be helpful to think of a lever. If someone wanted to move a large boulder, the person could place a block of wood next to the boulder, then position a long stick over the block of wood, with one end under the boulder. By pushing down on the other end of the stick, the person would be able to exert enough force against the boulder to move it. This is very similar to how one student of judo throws another.

The student in front has lowered his body to a kneeling position. He is about to stand up, while pulling his opponent forward. This way of using leverage enables students of judo to execute powerful throws.

By using the hips for leverage, a student can throw an opponent to the mat. This throw is the ogoshi, or "major hip throw."

An example of leverage in judo is the *ogoshi*, or "major hip throw." To execute the ogoshi, the student grasps his opponent and then spins around so that the student's back is toward the opponent. The student then uses the hips to lift the opponent off of the mat. The opponent can then be rolled off the student's back and thrown onto the mat.

LEG AND FOOT

TECHNIQUES

Though kicking is not a part of judo, leg and foot techniques are an important part of many throws. Students of judo use their legs and feet to push an opponent off-balance. This is sometimes done by sweeping the legs out from under the opponent, while pushing or pulling the opponent's upper body in the opposite direction.

An example of a leg technique is the *ouchigari,* or "major inner reaping throw." This throw begins with the student placing the right leg between the opponent's legs, while keeping the student's weight on the left leg. The student then hops toward the opponent, hooking the right leg around the opponent's left leg and pushing the opponent backwards. When done properly, the opponent will fall backwards to the mat.

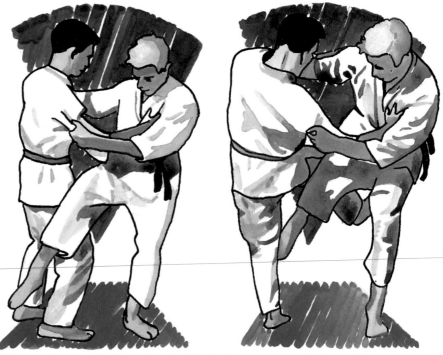

The student on the right is using his leg in an attempt to force his opponent off-balance. This throw is called the osotogari, *or "major outer reaping throw."*

Though the student on the left has fallen to the mat, he is still able to defeat his opponent by using the tomoenage, or "stomach throw."

In addition to being used to trip an opponent, the legs can also be used to throw an opponent. One example of the legs being used in a throw is the *tomoenage,* or "stomach throw." The tomoenage begins with the student falling to the mat, while hanging on to the opponent's lapels. Once on the mat, the student rolls onto his back and places a foot against the opponent's stomach. The leg is then used to throw the opponent up and over the student's head.

13

THE MENTAL EXERCISES: BREATHING AND

M
E
D
I
T
A
T
I
O
N

The word "judo" comes from the Japanese notion of *ju*. Ju can be thought of as the practice of *not* meeting force with force, or *not* reacting violently to the violence of an attacker. Understanding the notion of ju is important while training in judo. To be able to use the force of opponents against themselves, a student of judo must be able to concentrate.

To help students concentrate, they sit in *zazen* for a few minutes before beginning training. Zazen is a type of meditation that, when done properly, empties the mind of all thoughts not related to judo training. This helps a student to get the most out of every judo training session.

Proper breathing is also an important part of judo training. When practicing judo, students will often shout. They are not shouting because they are angry or excited. They are shouting in order to focus all of their physical and mental energies into the training. The shout is called a *kiai*. The breath for the kiai must come from deep in the abdomen. This gives the kiai more force.

At the end of each judo training session, the students sit in zazen again before leaving the dojo. This helps the students to remember all that they have learned in the training session.

Zazen, a type of meditation, is an important part of judo training.

JUDO

TODAY

Today, judo is a popular sport throughout the world, and is considered by many people to be the highest form of wrestling.

The international headquarters of judo is still the Kodokan in Tokyo, Japan. At the entrance of the Kodokan building is a statue of Jigoro Kano.

The International Judo Federation has hundreds of member nations. Almost every large community in the United States and Europe has at least one judo club, and the popularity of judo continues to grow. Judo is popular among both women and men.

Interest in judo, as both an Olympic sport and a means of physical fitness, is expected to increase during the 21st century.

Today, judo is considered to be the highest form of wrestling.

dan: the upper ranks in judo designated by a black, or higher ranking, belt.

dojo: a school of judo.

gi: a white judo uniform.

ju: the practice of *not* meeting force with force.

judoka: a student of judo.

kata: a series of rehearsed judo moves.

kiai: a loud yell that accompanies the execution of a judo technique.

Kodokan: the first school of judo; the international headquarters of judo.

kyu: the lower ranks in judo designated by the belt colors white, yellow, orange, green, blue and brown.

martial arts: any form of military training; often the term refers to empty-handed fighting, as well as to the various forms of exercises and sports developed from ancient fighting skills.

randori: free sparring done in judo training.

sensei: a teacher of judo.

taijutsu: an early form of Japanese unarmed fighting; samurai warriors trained in taijutsu.

ukemi: breakfall.

zazen: brief period of meditation at the beginning and end of a class in judo.

As well as providing a knowledge of self-defense, the practice of judo is also a popular form of physical exercise.

INDEX